YAS

FRIENDS
OF ACPL

S0-BSF-809

Political & Economic Systems

CAPITALISM

David Downing

Heinemann Library
Chicago, Illinois

Customer Service   888–454–2279

Visit our website at www.heinemannlibrary.com

Designed by AMR
Originated by Dot Gradations
Printed in Hong Kong by South China Printing

07 06 05 04 03
10 9 8 7 6 5 4 3 2 1

Library of Congress Cataloging-in-Publication Data

Downing, David, 1946 Aug. 9-
    Capitalism / David Downing.
        p. cm. -- (Political and economic systems)
    Includes bibliographical references and index.
    ISBN 1-40340-315-5
    1. Capitalism--Juvenile literature. [1. Capitalism.] I. Title. II.
Series.
    HB501 .D684 2003
    330.12'2--dc21
                                    2002006316

Acknowledgements
The publishers would like to thank the following for permission to reproduce photographs:
Rex/Nick Cobbins, p. 5; Corbis/Gianni Dagli Orti, p. 7; Bridgeman/Bristol Museum, p. 8;
Corbis/Bettmann, pp. 10, 11, 23, 24, 33; Corbis/Philip de Bay, p. 13; Hulton Archive/Lewis W.
Hine, p. 16; Hulton Archive/Gustave Dore, p. 17; Hulton Archive, pp. 18, 26, 29, 36, 41; Corbis,
p. 21; Hulton Archive/Dorothea Lange, p. 21; Corbis/Wally McNamee, p. 30; Rex/Andy Hernandez,
p. 34; Corbis/Charles O'Rear, p. 38; Corbis/David and Peter Turnley, p. 39; Corbis/Ecoscene, p. 43;
Corbis/Tony Arruza, p. 44; Corbis Sygma/Bob Daemmrich, p. 46; Corbis/Michael S. Yamashita,
p. 49; Corbis/Eye Ubiquitous, p. 50; Corbis/Keren Su, p. 52; Rex/Ray Tang, p. 54.

Cover photograph: Times Square, New York, reproduced with permission of Pictures Colour Library.

Our thanks to Christopher Gibb for his comments in the preparation of this book.

Some words are shown in bold, **like this.** You can find out what they
mean by looking in the glossary.

Contents

1 The Specter at the Feast

It was the last day of November in 1999 and the new millennium was only a month away. Ten years earlier, the power of world communism had collapsed, leaving the economic system known as capitalism in control of most of the globe. For over two centuries, capitalism had dominated the economic life of an ever-growing number of countries, making a lot of people very wealthy. People in the countries of the developed West were roughly twenty times better off than their ancestors had been in the 1750s.

There was surely nothing to complain about. Capitalism delivered the goods and the good life better than anyone could have expected. Yet on this day, in the beautiful city of Seattle, a wealthy city in the world's wealthiest country, a huge protest was taking place: a protest against capitalism.

Thousands of protesters marched down streets lined with stores full of all kinds of goods from all around the world. They marched in the shadows of huge modern skyscrapers that stood like monuments to capitalism's growth and prosperity. This was Seattle, famous for the TV sitcom *Frasier* and rock bands like Nirvana and Pearl Jam, proof that capitalism encouraged freedom and creativity. If any place on earth had been blessed by capitalism, then surely this was it. So why were these men and women marching?

Their banners told a confused story. Many were protesting against the **World Trade Organization,** whose meeting in the city had triggered the protest. Some carried signs condemning a general lack of justice and fairness in the world. Others had more particular targets in mind – logging companies that were cutting down forests, fast-food chains that seemed to be spreading like a virus around the world, industries that used animals to test the safety of their products. In the marchers' minds, all these issues were connected. As one Internet website advertising the event had put it, this was a global day of action and resistance against the global capitalist system.

No one doubted that capitalism had filled the shops with products and built the towering skyscrapers, but was it also responsible for the various problems and injustices that angered the protesters? What exactly was capitalism? Where had it come from, and how had it changed during the centuries of its rise to global domination? Why were some of those who had reaped its rewards now challenging it?

Police and protesters confront each other on the streets of Seattle in November of 1999. The protesters' sign is against the World Trade Organization (WTO).

② Where Did Capitalism Come From?

Capitalism is an economic system—a system that decides how goods and services are produced and traded. It has three key features: most property is owned by individuals; goods and services are exchanged in a competitive **free market** (one that is open to everyone); and **capital** (either money or other forms of wealth) is **invested** in businesses in order to make a **profit** (an increase in the wealth that was invested). Capitalism did not make a sudden appearance in world history. It developed slowly over several centuries and its importance grew within certain key societies until it dominated their economic life.

The seeds of capitalism

People have always owned things. Markets for trading goods have existed almost as long, and capital goods of both types—**working capital** and **fixed capital**—could be found in any primitive farm. The seeds saved from one year's harvest were the farmer's working capital, the raw material out of which he would create the next year's harvest. The hoe he used to plant those seeds was the farmer's fixed capital, the thing he needed to make the best use of his working capital. However, he was not using this capital to make a profit, only to feed himself and his family.

By the eleventh century there were an increasing number of merchants and traders using their fixed capital (a string of camels, perhaps) and working capital (maybe a shipment of silk) to make a profit.

Attitudes toward the creation of wealth

Before the triumph of capitalism, attitudes toward the creation of wealth were very different. In the Christian Bible it was said that: "...he who maketh haste [hurries] to be rich shall not be innocent" (Proverbs, chapter 28, verse 20). Other religions had the same distrust of those who sought wealth for its own sake. Such beliefs faded as capitalism became the dominant economic system, but as late as 1948, the Indian political and religious leader Mohandas Gandhi said that someone who charged as much as he possibly could for goods was no better than a thief. Attitudes like his are rare in today's world, but have not completely disappeared.

6

For several more centuries, these merchants played only a small part in the overall economy. The odds were stacked against people like this becoming more important. Medieval organizations of craftsmen and traders, called guilds, decided what the prices and wages would be in their towns, and this made it impossible for individuals to compete with each other by selling their goods or services more cheaply. There was also widespread religious prejudice against money-lending, which made it difficult for anyone to raise the capital needed to start or expand businesses. Those who did make profits would usually spend them on things like fine clothes and impressive houses, instead of using their money to make even more.

In this picture from a medieval book, an official from the Guild of Wool Merchants is paying a weaver for his cloth. The Guild controlled the weavers' rates of pay.

Commercial capitalism

Slowly but surely, as trade increased and the use of money spread, the small pockets of capitalistic activity in northern and western Europe grew in number and importance. In the fifteenth and sixteenth centuries, the vast expansion of trade that followed the opening up of routes to Asia and the newly discovered Americas introduced what became known as the age of commercial capitalism ("commerce" is another word for "trade"). Most of the capital was still **working capital**—the goods filling the ships then crossing the oceans—but there was also a large increase in those types of **fixed capital** that the new trade needed, like ships and dock facilities.

During the same period, there was an increase in the making of cloth in private homes. Merchants would deliver raw wool (the working capital) to households where primitive machines (the fixed capital) would be used to turn it into cloth. Arrangements like this were well on their way to full capitalism. Two hundred years later, textile-makers like these would be working full-time in heavily supervised factories for a wage.

This is a painting of Bristol, England in 1720. Ports like this one grew prosperous as world trade expanded under capitalism.

A more favorable climate

As capitalism's importance to the economies of these European countries grew, people's attitudes toward money and the creation of wealth also changed. Governments began to encourage their merchants and traders, and to support them against the merchants and traders of other countries. Businessmen grew more popular as the older ruling class—the land-owning **aristocracy**—grew less popular. This was also the period of the European **Enlightenment,** which placed a higher value on logical thinking and a lower one on stability. The climate for capitalism was suddenly looking better.

It was improved still further by the rise of **Protestantism,** which triggered the European **Reformation** of the sixteenth century. The work ethic of the Protestants made it much easier for capitalism to flourish.

The Industrial Revolution

In the eighteenth century, capitalism's takeover was speeded up even more by the series of inventions and technical advances that historians named the **Industrial Revolution.** The first industry to be transformed was the textile industry, in Britain. The invention and popularity of new machines like James Hargreaves' spinning-jenny (a machine that spun multiple threads into yarn much more quickly than could be done by hand) and Sir Richard Arkwright's water frame (a machine that used water power to produce cotton yarn) transformed what had been a part-time domestic activity— typically women working at home—into a paid factory job.

This new ability to make cheap cloth meant enormous **profits** for owners of the machines, and they invested their profits into new machines for making even more cloth. Traditional cloth producers, both in Britain and the rest of the world, struggled to compete, and by 1850 Britain's factories were making half the world's cotton goods.

This machine is a replica of the spinning frame invented by Richard Arkwright in the eighteenth century. It was used to spin wool into yarn and was much quicker than previous methods.

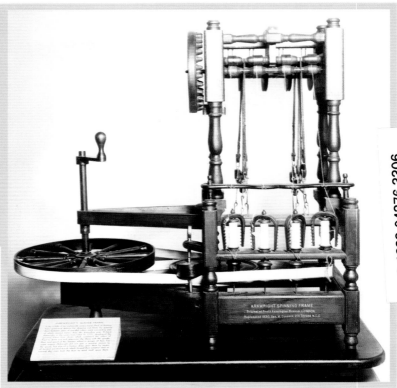

The same was true in industry after industry. The **fixed capital** of the late eighteenth and early nineteenth centuries (mines, ironworks, and potteries, for example) spread across the landscape of Europe and North America, turning **working capital** into profits. These profits were continually reinvested in more **capital,** which almost always meant more profits. By the mid-nineteenth century, capitalism grew quickly to become the dominant force in all these economies.

③ Building Prosperity

In the late eighteenth century, the Scottish **philosopher** and economist Adam Smith wrote a book called *An Inquiry into the Nature and Causes of the Wealth of Nations*. In this book he explained how capitalism worked and why he believed it worked in the interests of everyone, not just those fortunate enough to own capital. If certain conditions were met, he said, and if most property was private and people were able to choose between competing buyers and sellers in a **free market,** then one person's pursuit of profit would end up benefiting not just himself but the whole community. What Smith called the "invisible hand" of the market would work in everyone's interests.

Adam Smith (1723–1790) was a Scottish economist and philosopher. Many people consider him to be the founder of modern economics.

How capitalism works

Why would one person's profit not be someone else's loss? According to Smith, it worked something like this. A businessman (businesswomen were almost unheard of at the time) would borrow the money to buy the machines that he needed to set up a factory for making a product, like wool blankets. The cost of making each blanket—what the businessman had to pay—would include **interest payments** on his loan, wages to his workers, rent or mortgage on his factory, energy costs, and expenditure (what he spent) on raw materials like wool and dyes. In order to make a **profit,** he had to charge his customers more for his blankets than the amount it had cost him to make them.

So why would this businessman not charge twice the cost and make himself a huge profit? Adam Smith's answer was simple: he could not do so because he was competing in a **free market** with other blanket manufacturers. If he raised his prices too high, and tried to make too much profit, then people would buy blankets from his competitors, who were charging less. Competition kept prices down.

In order to compete, the businessman was involved in a relentless effort to keep his costs down. It was in his best interest to make his blanket business more efficient by using better machines and fewer workers. If he did not, and his competitors did, then he would be unable to sell his overpriced blankets.

This search for profit drove capitalism forward. Businessmen in every industry struggled to undercut their competitors by finding new ways of making things, new things to make that people wanted, new markets at home and abroad to sell them in, anything at all to give them an advantage. The outcome was a whole new world of mass-produced, cheaper products.

The golden age

During the first half of the nineteenth century, capitalism developed the way Smith had said it would. Most businesses were owned by the individuals or families who ran them, and not, as is usually the case today, by thousands of **shareholders** who are not involved in the day-to-day operations. Most businesses were also small by today's standards, and the fierce and open competition between them benefited the consumer.

The people of the time believed in saving most of their wealth, which encouraged investment. They also admired those who were prepared to take the risk of trying something new, which encouraged innovation.

This was the golden age of capitalism. In 1851, the Great Exhibition was held in London to celebrate progress. Thousands of people came to see the amazing machines that had transformed the way they lived. Even people who did not agree with the ideas of capitalism were stunned by the enormity of the changes. Three years earlier, in their **Communist** *Manifesto*, Karl Marx and Friedrich Engels had written that "capitalism, during its rule of scarce [barely] one hundred years, has created more massive and more colossal productive forces [more machines for making goods] than have all preceding generations together."

FOR INFORMATION ON KEY PEOPLE, SEE PAGES 59–60.

Visitors to the Great Exhibition in London, in 1851, marvel at the new machines on display.

There was no slackening of the pace in the second half of the nineteenth century. The rise of new industries based on oil and electricity, and the development of automobiles and manned flight, all changed the face of the land and the way people lived their lives. By the time World War I broke out in August of 1914, only small pockets of the old, slow-moving, pre-industrial world still existed in Europe and North America. In its place, the capitalist growth machine had built a prosperous world of cities and speeding machines, a world in which fast-growing economies went hand in hand with spreading education, widening **democracy,** and flourishing culture.

Stock markets and shareholders

Businesspeople often needed extra capital to make their businesses grow faster. At the same time there were many private investors with small amounts of capital who were interested in making a **profit.** So a system developed in which businesspeople sold the investors **shares** in their businesses, and paid them a share of whatever profits they eventually made. These shares were bought and sold in a market called a stock exchange. As individual ownership of businesses declined, and most came to be owned by thousands of shareholders, stock exchanges like those on Wall Street in New York City became vital centers of the capitalist economy.

4 The Dark Side

Capitalism's tremendous success was enjoyed by many people, particularly in Europe and North America. But by the end of the nineteenth century, doubts were beginning to grow. Many people had paid a terrible price for the wealth that had been created, and capitalism itself had moved far beyond the simplicity described by Adam Smith.

> FOR INFORMATION ON KEY PEOPLE, SEE PAGES 59–60.

A different world

In the new industrial world, working conditions were usually unhealthy, the machinery was sometimes dangerous, and the air was full of poisons. For the first time in history, millions of people were working fixed hours under the constant supervision of others. Few of them had any say in what they were making, how quickly they worked, or what happened to the product after they had made it. They began to feel like a part of a huge machine.

Some owners and managers tried to improve conditions for their workers, and to treat them like fellow human beings, but under capitalism the need for **profits** usually came first. If a capitalist business needed to cut its costs in order to compete, then lowering wages or laying off workers was sometimes the best way to reduce them. Because workers needed to be close to the industrial centers, they were unable to feed themselves by growing vegetables or keeping animals. They were now completely dependent on their wages, and at the mercy of their bosses.

Dark times

"It was a town of machinery and tall chimneys, out of which interminable serpents of smoke trailed themselves for ever and ever, and never got uncoiled. It had a black canal in it, and a river that ran purple with ill-smelling dye, and vast piles of building full of windows where there was a rattling and a trembling all day long, and where the piston of the steam-engine worked monotonously up and down like the head of an elephant in a state of melancholy madness."

(Charles Dickens describing the fictional Coketown in *Hard Times*, his novel about the horrors of the **Industrial Revolution**.)

Of course, when more members of a family were able to work, the family was able to bring home more money. In the early years of capitalism, women and children had to work long hours in terrible conditions because that was the only way they could find the means to live. The system thrived on their cheap labor, and a resentment of the system began to grow. Capitalism was producing wealth beyond the wildest dreams of earlier centuries, but it was ending up in far fewer pockets than seemed fair. Too many people were living their lives in a constant state of insecurity, poverty, and poor health.

This photograph was taken in a cotton mill in Georgia in the early twentieth century. These two young boys would have worked long hours for low pay.

The market grows less free

During the second half of the nineteenth century, many working people came to support measures for reforming capitalism. They demanded improved working conditions, a larger share of the profits, and better legal rights. They argued that governments should give **benefits** to those who were unable to work, either because they were too old or because there were not enough jobs to go around.

They formed **trade unions** to press their demands on employers and **socialist** political parties to press their arguments on governments. At the end of the nineteenth and beginning of the twentieth centuries, this pressure began to pay off. Old age pensions and **unemployment benefits** were introduced in many of the richer countries.

These nineteenth-century workers' houses in London, England, were crammed together under the smoking chimneys of the nearby factory.

This pressure from workers pushed wages higher than they would have gone in a truly free market. At the same time, their employers were finding that they could raise their prices higher than a free market would have allowed. During the second half of the nineteenth century, the size of businesses increased, leaving fewer and fewer left standing. As a result, there was less real competition. When only three blanket manufacturers were left in the market, it was relatively easy for their bosses to reach a secret agreement on what price they would all charge. There were attempts to prevent companies from acting together in this way, like the American **anti-trust laws** of the 1890s, but they were not always effective.

17

Factory work was often extremely boring. These women working in a factory in Liverpool, England, during the 1920s, are coating cookies with colored sugar.

Trade between nations was also taking place in an increasingly un-free market. Great Britain, for example, was eager to promote free trade between nations. Their products were cheaper and well-made, and would sell well abroad. For nations struggling to catch up, however, the opposite was true. In order to protect their own infant industries while they grew, these nations adopted a protectionist policy that stifled free trade and, as a result, hurt international relations.

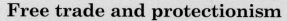

Free trade and protectionism

In a **free market,** the most efficient businesses prosper and the least efficient usually fail. In international terms, this might mean that country A's efficient steel industry would prosper and country B's inefficient one would fail, leaving steel consumers in country B to buy their steel from country A. The government of country A would be happy about this; its workers would be fully employed and its steel exports would be earning money for the country. Where steel was concerned, country A would be in favor of a free international market, or free trade.

The government of country B would not be happy. All of its steel workers would be unemployed and it would be paying for foreign steel. It would probably prefer to protect its own steel industry by charging a fee, or **tariff,** on each ton of steel that country A tried to bring in. This would make country A's steel more expensive than it really was in country B, and allow country B's industry to compete in its own market. The use of such tariffs to protect home industries is called protectionism.

By 1900, the free market envisioned by Adam Smith had all but disappeared, and capitalism was beginning to encounter serious problems. It was still showing an amazing ability to create wealth, but it was also responsible for encouraging serious conflicts, both within and between nations.

5 The Crises of Capitalism

World War I threw the world economy off balance. Some countries, like Britain, France, and Germany, had been badly hurt by the financial cost of fighting the war, while others, like the United States and Japan, had prospered. The decision by the victorious countries to make Germany pay **reparations** as a punishment for starting the war made matters worse, and by the early 1920s the West European economies were in deep trouble. Many people hoped that capitalism was capable of sorting itself out without interference from the politicians.

The Great Depression

This did not happen. Between 1925 and 1928 the developed economies showed signs of growth. However, there were already signs of a slowdown in the United States when the **Great Crash** on the stock market in October of 1929 triggered a collapse in the country's economy. This led to a shrinking of the entire world economy—because the United States had become the global economic leader—which became known as the **Great Depression.** In the years that followed, thousands of companies around the world went bankrupt, millions of workers became unemployed, and trade collapsed. It seemed as if capitalism's growth machine had gone into reverse. Instead of success creating success, failure bred failure.

Capitalism no longer looked like a system that worked and, for some, it even began to look like a system that was morally wrong. How, people asked, could one justify pouring away milk that hungry people needed, just because they had no money to pay for it? Many critics pointed to the **communist** and **fascist** countries, which seemed at the time to be coping with the Great Depression much better than capitalist countries were.

Post-war blues

"It is not intelligent. It is not beautiful. It is not just. It is not virtuous. And it doesn't deliver the goods."

(English economist John Maynard Keynes, describing international capitalism in the aftermath of World War I.)

This photo shows a line of unemployed men in San Francisco during the Great Depression.

Regulating capitalism

Faced with the Great Depression, the governments of the leading democratic countries—the United States, Great Britain, France, and Germany—waited in vain for capitalism to straighten itself out. When it became clear that it was not going to happen, they began listening to capitalism's critics, who believed that the governments themselves needed to straighten it out.

One of the best-known of these critics was John Maynard Keynes, a British economist. He had long argued that the perfect capitalism of the free market described by Adam Smith no longer existed. Businesses and **trade unions** had been able to keep prices and wages high.

This had stopped the market from working as it should, and made it impossible for capitalism to regulate itself. Capitalism was like a boat with a broken rudder. It could still move quickly, but it needed help steering a straight course.

FOR INFORMATION ON KEY PEOPLE, SEE PAGES 59–60.

Only governments could provide that help. If they spent money when the economy was doing badly—as it was in the Great Depression—then that would encourage growth.

The British economist John Maynard Keynes (1883–1946) was one of the first people to argue that capitalism needed regulating.

At other times, when the economy was doing too well and threatening to grow too fast, governments could raise **taxes** and **interest rates** to slow growth down. In such ways, capitalism could be made more predictable and more reliable.

The first government to test out this theory of regulation was the U.S. administration headed by President Franklin D. Roosevelt, who was in office from 1933 to 1945. It worked. The spending programs known as the New Deal kick-started the U.S. economy back into motion and slowly put the nation back to work.

The New Deal

The New Deal was the name given to the programs put in place by the Roosevelt administration to overcome the Great Depression through the spending of government money. Millions of unemployed men and women were paid by the government to do a variety of tasks, including building new houses and dams, electrifying railroads, planting new forests, even picking up leaves. The money that they were paid was spent on goods, which helped other businesses get back on their feet. Slowly, the economy began to grow again.

It was World War II that mopped up the last unemployment left by the Great Depression, but the capitalist world as a whole had now adopted Keynes's ideas. Once the war was over, most governments began to carefully manage and regulate their national economies. In Europe many large private businesses were taken into **public ownership** and run by the government. In both the United States and Europe, large increases in government spending, paid for by government borrowing, were used to stimulate the economy.

The result was a return to growth. Between 1950 and the early 1970s, the regulated capitalist economies (including a newly revived West Germany and Japan) boomed, their industrial outputs increasing as much as four times. New industries like plastics and electronics grew rapidly, keeping unemployment low. In many countries, governments used high tax **revenues** to pay for increasing health and **welfare benefits.** The growth machine was back on track, and this time it seemed to have a more caring side. This new welfare capitalism was a system that not only produced wealth but also looked after all of its people.

By the 1950s, the capitalist economies were booming and consumers had money to spend on new household goods, such as this washing machine.

A new crisis

The post-war boom lasted until the early 1970s, when the economies of the developed world found they were suffering from something Keynes had believed impossible—a combination of high **inflation** and high unemployment.

There was no single obvious cause for this problem, and economists disagreed about how important the various causes were. Some said it was because of the rise in oil prices that followed an Arab–Israeli War in 1973. Some thought it was because the United States had borrowed money to pay for the Vietnam War (1963–1975). Others pointed to the high level of government spending, which was needed to pay for the welfare benefits that people now took for granted.

Whatever the cause, capitalism seemed to be failing once again. More and more people were losing their jobs and goods were becoming more expensive. The crisis was not as desperate as it had been in the 1930s, and this time around there was nothing left to challenge capitalism. **Fascism** was a disgraced memory, and it was becoming very obvious that **communism** was unable to create the sort of highly developed economy that existed under capitalism.

During the 1970s, oil prices rose steeply and there were several scares about shortages in supplies. Service stations like this one in California were jammed with cars as people tried to stock up on gasoline.

Deregulating capitalism

Capitalism's answer to this crisis was to turn its back on the idea of regulation. The influential economists of the 1970s, such as Milton Friedman and Friedrich von Hayek (both of whom won the Nobel Prize for economics in that decade), argued for a return to a purer, unregulated capitalism. They wanted governments to create the conditions for pure competition (one way to do this would be to weaken the power of unions to keep wages higher), and then step back.

Versions of these theories were put into practice by the governments of Ronald Reagan in the United States and Margaret Thatcher in Great Britain. They put many state-owned companies back into private ownership **(privatization),** introduced laws to weaken the unions, and tried to cut government spending, especially on welfare. Their example was followed by many governments around the world, although in continental Europe there was more resistance to the reduction of welfare benefits. By 1990, when communism suddenly collapsed in eastern Europe, capitalism was more than triumphant—it was reliving the glory days of the nineteenth century. And, similar to what happened before, the last decade of the twentieth century was marked by rapid growth and an increase in inequality, both within and between nations.

6 The Politics of Capitalism

Capitalism is a type of economic system. As we have seen, it can have profound social consequences. It has changed the way we work and greatly altered the overall distribution of wealth. But what political consequences has it had? How has capitalism changed the way countries are governed?

Liberalism

Adam Smith believed that the **free market** worked best when left to itself. He felt that any form of government intervention was, at best, a necessary evil. He understood that governments needed to provide certain things—like public schools, the armed forces, and the legal system—that the market could not. However, he insisted that its only other economic role was to remove any and all restrictions on the working of the market.

This desire to free, or liberalize, the workings of the market was the driving power behind **liberalism,** the dominant political force of early nineteenth-century capitalism. Liberals wanted to help capitalism overcome obstacles such as outdated restrictions on certain types of economic activity, or the continuing power of the monarchs, the church, and the land-owning **aristocrats,** who felt threatened by the rise of the new capitalist class.

In order to change these regulations, and to override the power of the ruling classes, the new liberalizing capitalists needed to

This painting shows a mob burning down a farm in Kent in protest against the British Corn Laws. These laws, which prevented a free market in grain, were eventually repealed in 1846.

promote and strengthen the **democratic** institutions that already existed in Europe and North America (because in most cases, leaders were only elected by a small, property-owning portion of the male population: no one else had the right to vote). These strengthened institutions could then be used to make life easier for capitalism.

Some of the liberal changes were good for everyone. Getting rid of taxes on newspapers, for example, led to cheaper papers and a wider spread of information. This helped businessmen make profitable decisions and increased the information available to ordinary citizens.

But other measures were not as good for the masses. Giving money to the poor was discouraged, because it was believed that it would keep them from wanting to work, and trade unions were outlawed because they gave the workers more power. The liberals of the time thought that both charity and trade unions interfered with the free working of the capitalist market.

Capitalism and slavery

The early nineteenth-century drive to abolish slavery, largely led by the new liberal middle class, was a good example of how and why capitalism encouraged the spread of liberty. There were many individual capitalists who objected to slavery on moral grounds, but from Adam Smith's point of view the main problem with slavery was that it interfered with the free working of the labor market. Capitalism needed free workers, who could move from place to place and change jobs, if the free market was to operate efficiently.

Socialism

As the nineteenth century unfolded, it appeared that capitalism's ability to create wealth was matched by its tendency to divide up the wealth unequally. Those with **capital** to **invest** always made more money than those people who could not afford to save any money to invest. Governments offered a little help to those on the bottom rungs of the economic ladder. For example, the employment of children under the age of nine was banned in Britain by the Factory Act of 1833. However, the resentment toward capitalism continued to grow, and in the second half of the century it found a political voice in the growth of trade unions and **socialist** parties.

The basic argument of these political groups was that when left to itself, capitalism caused too much misery to too many people. They agreed that capitalism was an excellent producer of wealth, but claimed that it was not able to make sure that everyone received a fair share. If capitalism itself could not do this, then governments had to. Socialists believed that governments had to take a more active role in the economy for the sake of the people as a whole.

There were several ways that governments could do this. They could pay old age pensions to people who were too old to keep working and they could pay **unemployment benefits** to those who could not find work. They could tax the rich more heavily and use the money they got from this to make life more comfortable for the poor. They could even take unprofitable industries into public ownership and use taxpayers' money to keep them afloat. This protected the jobs of the people who worked in them. They could do some or all of these things, but each one of them meant an intervention in the free working of the market.

The twentieth century

The politics of capitalism in the twentieth century revolved around the question of how much intervention there should be. A few extremists still argued for the total lack of intervention suggested by Adam Smith, while twentieth-century **communists** argued for the maximum amount of intervention—the ending of the **free market** and almost complete government control over all economic activity. However, most political debate has been between those on the moderate **right,** who favor a little intervention, and those on the moderate **left,** who would like to see more government intervention.

Those on the moderate right have argued that too much government intervention threatens individual freedom and makes capitalism less efficient. These people claim that a free, efficient capitalism is in everyone's best interest because it produces more wealth for people to share, no matter how unfair the actual sharing may be. Those on the moderate left, however, have argued that more government intervention would make up for capitalism's natural tendency to promote inequality, and could help to create a fairer, more **democratic** society. The outcome, they believe, would be well worth any small loss in personal freedom or economic efficiency that might result.

In general, the moderate left won this argument between the 1930s and the early 1970s. In both North America and

A poster at Waterloo Station in London, England, announces that Britain's railroads have been taken over by the state. This was one way that a government could intervene in the economy, protecting workers' jobs and public services.

29

Europe, government intervention in capitalist economies was far more common after the Great Depression than it had been before. But the situation was reversed during the last quarter of the twentieth century. The moderate **right** took control, and government intervention in most developed countries was systematically reduced.

There is no reason to assume that this latest preference will last forever. The very nature of capitalism—its ability to generate both great wealth and great unfairness—means that this political argument, between those who put wealth first and those who put fairness first, will continue as long as capitalism exists as an economic system.

FOR INFORMATION ON KEY PEOPLE, SEE PAGES 59–60.

During the 1980s, President Ronald Reagan and British Prime Minister Margaret Thatcher both took steps to restrict the role of government in their countries' economies.

Capitalism and democracy

Some people have argued, and many others believe, that **free market** capitalism and **democracy** were made for each other. This is not necessarily true. Throughout capitalism's golden age in the nineteenth-century, the number of adults who were allowed to vote was strictly limited. **Universal suffrage** was only introduced in the richer countries in the twentieth century, and some capitalist countries, such as Saudi Arabia, still don't allow all of its adult citizens to vote.

In developed countries, certain features of capitalism have leaned towards democracy. For capitalism to work, individuals must have economic freedom, so political freedom seems like the natural next step. However, other aspects of capitalism have worked against democracy, especially its ability to create inequality. The political equality of one person (one vote) means a lot less when just a few people have so much more economic power than others.

Capitalism and freedom

Capitalism and freedom are often linked together, as if they were the same thing. This is only partly true. Capitalism needs a free market—that is, one in which governments do not try to interfere in the buying and selling of goods and services. It also relies on a spirit of free enterprise, on individual ambition, and initiative. It requires what **philosophers** have called the "freedoms to"—to trade and to speak one's mind, for example—the freedoms that allow people to do what they individually want to do within agreed rules of law.

However, capitalism does not need all of the political freedoms that are generally enjoyed in early twenty-first-century North America and Europe in order to operate. It has worked perfectly well in a variety of political environments—such as **colonialism**, civil and military **dictatorships**, even communist dictatorships like present-day China—in which political freedoms have been severely limited. And in many cases, capitalism has failed to make room for what philosophers call the "freedoms from," such as freedom from hunger, freedom from unemployment, and freedom from insecurity and fear.

Communism: Capitalism's Enemy?

Capitalism faced two major challenges in the twentieth century. The first of these came from within. It involved reforming and regulating itself to the point where it became acceptable to a large majority of the population. The second, the challenge of **communism,** came from outside. This second challenge was political, economic, and, at times, even came from a military.

Communism comes to power

Communism was a response to capitalism's failure in certain parts of the world. In Russia, where the first communist revolution took place in October of 1917, capitalism's dark side—the horrible working conditions and the growing inequalities—had become painfully obvious. Few people had benefited from capitalism's ability to create wealth. Much of the capital invested in Russia before World War I had come from other countries, and few of the **profits** were seen by ordinary Russians. When Vladimir Ilyich Lenin's victorious Communist Party announced that they intended to abolish capitalism and create a kind of **socialism** in its place, most Russians were glad.

Similar chains of events took place in China and Cuba, too. Before their revolutions—in 1949 and 1959 respectively—both countries experienced many of capitalism's negative points and only a few of its positive points, and both countries were willing, at least in the beginning, to try and create something different.

Abolishing capitalism

The Russian communists abolished capitalism. Private ownership of most property was ended, leaving no way for a competitive free market to exist. All economic decisions, such as what to produce and how to produce it, were now made by the "visible hand" of government

FOR INFORMATION ON KEY PEOPLE, SEE PAGES 59–60.

instead of what Adam Smith called the "invisible hand" of the free market. The government planners decided to invest in a new steel mill or a new dam because they thought the country needed these things, not because they expected to make a profit out of them.

The communists claimed that this was both more rational (only the things that were really needed got produced) and fairer. There were no capitalists at the top enjoying all of the wealth, and no workers at the bottom, slaving away for someone else.

This was not entirely true. It turned out that economic planning only worked well in the early stages of industrialization. Once the economy grew more complicated, the "visible hand" of government proved to be much more clumsy and inefficient than the "invisible hand" of the market. It also turned out that, with or without profits, those who ran the system still managed to enjoy an unfair share of what was produced. In reality, communism was no fairer than capitalism.

The message on this propaganda poster from the Russian Revolution says: "You still haven't joined the Cooperative—sign up immediately!"

Finally, and perhaps most importantly of all, the lack of economic freedom also came with a lack of political freedom. Creativity, innovation, and individual ambition and enthusiasm were all stifled. Communism lacked all of those things that had turned capitalism into a growth machine.

Lenin on capitalism

"Capitalists are no more capable of self-sacrifice than a man is capable of lifting himself up by his own bootstraps."

(Russian communist leader Vladimir Lenin, stating his belief that, under capitalism, the rich did not want to help the poor and the poor were unable to help themselves.)

Cold War

The problems with communism took a long time to become obvious. In the 1930s, when the leading capitalist countries were suffering from the the Great Depression, communist Russia seemed to be forging ahead with its ambitious **five-year plans.** The level of suffering in the West was well-known, but the much greater level of suffering in Russia was hardly known at all. Russian military success in World War II and the amazing economic recovery that followed only heightened the reputation of the communists.

During the final years of the communist Soviet Union, there were shortages of many goods. People often had to wait in line for hours just to buy food.

By 1950, the capitalist world had fully recovered. During the first twenty years of the **Cold War** (1948–1968), each of the two systems tried to prove that it was better than the other. Capitalism and communism also competed for influence in the developing countries of Asia, Africa, and Latin America, where the capitalist world was at a disadvantage. For one thing, the capitalist countries were considered responsible for the poverty that existed throughout the developing world. Secondly, communism seemed good at providing the sort of basic economic development that many of the poorer countries so desperately needed. It had worked for Russia and China, so why couldn't it work for other undeveloped countries?

Eventually, though, the communist countries' failure to produce a wide range of goods that their own people wanted (goods that people in the advanced capitalist countries took for granted) resulted in the collapse of European communism. It also resulted in the end—in all but name—of communism in east Asia. By 1991, capitalism's dominance over communism around the globe was virtually complete.

The only sour note was the continuing poverty of many developing countries. It was this human suffering that had produced so much hostility in those countries toward capitalism, and had generated so much support for communism.

⑧ Capitalism and the Poorer Countries

The enormous wealth that capitalism generated during the nineteenth and twentieth centuries was not spread evenly across the globe. Some countries were much richer than others, and inside all countries a few people were much richer than others. As the twentieth century ended, these gaps kept growing wider. Almost a quarter of the world's people (most of them living in the world's poorest countries) had an income of less than $370.00 a year. Clearly, capitalism was not working very well for these people.

Colonialism and after

Some people blamed this situation on **colonialism,** the rule of poor, undeveloped countries by economically advanced countries. They claimed that European powers like Great Britain and France—which had ruled large parts of the world for several centuries—had held back those countries that they occupied.

This painting shows British ships lining the docks at the port of Calcutta in India during the days of the British Empire.

Instead of giving or selling modern technology to these countries, letting them create their own industrial revolution, the colonial powers had used these countries as sources of raw materials and markets for their own products. Great Britain, for example, had arranged taxes and **tariffs** in a way that allowed their own cotton manufacturers to outsell Indian cotton manufacturers—even in India!

Supporters of colonialism have argued that colonial systems improved the conditions of the countries they occupied. They often left them with better roads, railroads, and docks. Whether or not those advances outweigh the negative after-effects of colonialism, however, is debatable.

Most direct colonial rule came to an end during the second half of the twentieth century. However, those most critical of the rich countries' behavior in the "third" (or developing) world argue that not much had changed. Countries were given political independence, but they were still economically dependent on the richer countries. The World Bank and International Monetary Fund were supposed to provide help, but they were effectively controlled by the United States and the old colonial powers.

Overseeing the international economy

There are three major international economic organizations. The International Bank for Reconstruction and Development (known as the World Bank) and the International Monetary Fund (IMF) were both formed in 1945 to encourage world economic development. Both have loaned large amounts of money to developing countries, many of which have not been able to repay those loans. In the late 1990s, a worldwide campaign was launched to cancel many of the outstanding debts.

The **World Trade Organization (WTO)** was founded in 1995 as the successor to the General Agreement on Tariffs and Trade (GATT). Its main task is to regulate trade and, where possible, remove barriers to free trade. Since free trade tends to benefit the richer, more efficient producing countries, the WTO has been subject to criticism and protest.

According to capitalism's critics, people and businesses in the richer countries held on to most of the economic power. They decided where to invest their capital in new businesses and jobs. The poorer countries, had to accept whatever they were offered. They had little bargaining power of their own.

Not surprisingly, capitalism's supporters had a more positive view of its record in the developing world. They pointed to the success of what were called the **"Asian Tigers"**—countries like South Korea, Taiwan, Singapore, and Malaysia—that had managed to lift themselves out of poverty by stressing education and hard work and by keeping wages low. These countries had successfully competed with the rich nations by doing exactly what Adam Smith would have recommended. They had made products that the richer nations wanted more cheaply and efficiently than the rich nations could do it themselves.

This assembly plant in Durban, South Africa, is owned by the Japanese company Toyota. Multinational corporations like Toyota provide jobs for people in many of the world's poorer countries.

Opting out

The most important change to affect the international economy over the last 25 years has been the rise of **multinational corporations.** These businesses, which conduct operations all over the world, can have more money than some national governments. Their supporters have claimed that they bring new technology, new management methods, and new jobs to the poorer countries, and should therefore be welcomed. Their critics argued that the jobs are few, the major decisions are all made at corporate headquarters in the rich countries, and that most of the profits are sent home. These critics have claimed that the multinational corporations are only using them as a source of cheap labor, and have not done anything to develop the poorer countries.

In order to protect themselves from the overwhelming power of foreign economic interests, some of the poorer countries have tried to opt out of the world capitalist system. In the early 1960s, for example, Cuba joined the **communist** world when its revolutionary leaders realized that staying in the capitalist system would mean domination by the nearby United States. Also in the 1960s, President Julius Nyerere of Tanzania tried to introduce a form of socialism in semi-isolation from the capitalist world. Other developing countries have also made occasional attempts to try it alone.

There have been some successes: Cuba's system of health care, for example, is considered to be the best in Latin America. Generally speaking, however, the attempts made by small countries to step outside the capitalist system have failed. Capitalism has been too powerful for them in almost every respect. Its economic success has been impossible to ignore, and its economic (and sometimes its military) power have been impossible to resist.

These women and children in Egypt survive by rummaging through a dump in search of food and things to sell. Critics of multinational corporations claim that they usually do not bring wealth to the poorer countries where their factories are based.

Extending welfare capitalism?

Over the last hundred years the whole world has learned what Europe and North America learned in the nineteenth century—that capitalism can create both wealth and inequality. The European and North American answer was to regulate and reform capitalism to the point where it offered something for everyone, even those at the bottom of the economic ladder. If the widening gap between rich and poor countries is to be narrowed, it seems likely that something similar will need to be introduced internationally. How this can be achieved without having an international government is one of the most important questions facing people and politicians in the twenty-first century.

⑨ Capitalism and the Environment

Even if capitalism managed to raise the economic level of the world's poorer countries to that enjoyed by the richer countries, it would, unfortunately, find itself with another problem. Experts have estimated that this level of worldwide economic growth would demand a five-time increase in energy consumption. At this time, the current levels of energy use are already creating major problems for the environment.

Dark beginnings

As early as 1804, the British writer William Blake contrasted the dark, dangerous mills of the **Industrial Revolution** with the green, pleasant land they were replacing. As the century unfolded, things only got worse. Each year thousands of new factories in western Europe and North America coughed coal smoke and unhealthy gases into the air, darkening the daytime sky over rapidly growing towns.

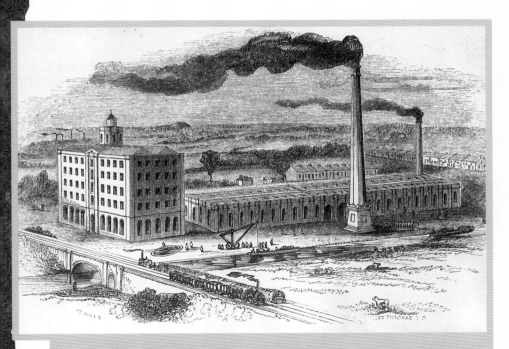

This painting from 1840 shows a newly built metalworks in England. The writer William Blake was critical of the way that factories like this one were spoiling the English countryside.

41

Most governments did not make any attempts to limit this poisoning of the air and water with industrial waste. For well over a century, capitalist industry was allowed to make its profits without cleaning up after itself.

Things began to change around the middle of the twentieth century. The areas affected by industrial pollution had slowly grown, and now included large parts of the most developed countries. For example, London, the capital of England, experienced serious smog (industrial fogs) in the early 1950s. One of them is believed to have killed several hundred people. Both in London and elsewhere a serious effort was made to clean up industry. This was made easier by the fact that coal-fueled industries were, in many cases, already giving way to alternatives that caused less pollution.

Limits to growth?

The next major environmental crisis came in the mid-1970s. Experts claimed that the world's population was increasing too quickly, and that at current rates the world would soon exhaust its stocks of raw materials—like oil and minerals—which could not be replaced. They argued that there was a limit to growth, and that capitalism, which seemed unable to stand still, would need to change. By the end of the twentieth century, however, the expected shortages had not happened. New experts claimed that they never would, that capitalism's restless spirit would always find new new ways of doing things when old ones no longer worked.

But there were still many doubters. They pointed to signs like the continuing destruction of the rainforests, and stressed the risks humanity was facing by using up its resources so quickly.

This area of Malaysian rainforest has been cleared of trees to make way for agriculture. Environmental experts are worried that cutting down rainforests may be contributing to global warming.

In the meantime, other dangers of headlong growth were becoming apparent. The most important of these was **global warming.** According to scientists, a steady rise in the amount of industrial emissions pumped into the air was raising the global temperature. This can cause serious consequences for sea levels and local climates. Once again, many voices were insisting that capitalism's growth had to be slowed down or even stopped.

Capitalism's problem?

It could be argued that industrialism, not capitalism, was responsible for these problems. The **communist** world's environmental record had been just as bad, if not worse. By the end of the twentieth century, though, capitalism was responsible for almost all of the world's industrial growth, and almost all of the environmental problems that this growth created. So was capitalism a good system for putting things right?

43

Adam Smith's argument, that individuals pursuing their own individual interests will end up benefiting everyone, clearly does not work where the environment is concerned. Factory owners who lowered their costs by dumping poisonous waste in the river are helping themselves while harming the community. Their competitors are then encouraged to do the same, because that is the only way they can compete. The only way around this is for governments to pass laws against such behavior, and then enforce those laws.

This can work within countries, but when thinking about the world at large, it is much harder to agree on or enforce these regulations. In 2001, the United States decided to withdraw from the 1997 Kyoto Agreement on limiting the emissions that lead to global warming. This was an indication of how hard it may be, in a competitive, capitalist world, to persuade nations to set aside their own self-interests for the interests of the world as a whole.

A traffic jam contributes to the global warming problem.

Capitalism's solutions?

There has been a huge growth in the sale of so-called green products (such as enzyme-free detergents, long-life light bulbs, and electric cars) that are environmentally friendly. Governments have encouraged the recycling of garbage, and there has been a steep rise in the practice of charging both businesses and individuals for the damage they do to the environment. Factory owners, who at one time just dumped their waste in a river and thought nothing of it, now have to pay for safe disposal or face heavy fines.

Toll roads

Toll roads are a good example of how, under capitalism, polluters can be made to pay for the pollution they cause. If car owners are charged for using city streets they will use their cars less, which will lower the level of exhaust emissions. When they do choose to pay the charges and use their cars, the money collected can be used to improve public transportation. Once public transportation is improved, more people will choose to use it, and this will lessen pollution even more. In the meantime, the high cost of using cars that pollute will have created a new and growing market for cars that do not.

Measures like these include the cost of preserving the environment in the overall cost of goods and services, thus raising the prices. Supporters of capitalism believe that this will be enough to solve the world's environmental problems. They claim that there is no need for serious reforms or to abandon capitalism. Others believe that this approach, if it works at all, will work far too slowly. They believe that the environmental crisis facing the capitalist world of the twenty-first century is every bit as serious as that which faced capitalism in the 1930s, and argue that it will only be overcome by governmental intervention on a large scale.

Globalization

In the last decade of the twentieth century, capitalism nearly took over the entire international economy. The end of **communism** in Europe and, at the same time, the opening up of communist China to capitalist enterprise, were two reasons for this globalization, but they were not the only ones. Advances in telecommunications and computers, which meant that the whole world could be reached quickly and easily, and the growth of **multinational corporations** which make use of these advances, were even more important.

In the 1980s and 1990s, many restrictions on international trade were lifted and the multinational corporations were able to start moving their capital around the world in search of the best deals. Not surprisingly, they often chose to set up their operations in poorer countries like Mexico and Indonesia, where workers earning cheaper salaries would bring down the cost of production. It also made sense for some of these corporations to hire local firms to do the actual manufacturing. That way, the corporation would not have to pay the local workers unemployment or health benefits.

Workers in Austin, Texas, demonstrate against the North American Free Trade Agreement in November of 1993. Many are afraid that companies will move their operations to Mexico, where wages are lower. This protester's sign reads "Down with NAFTA."

Consequences for the richer countries

Capitalism's globalization has had important consequences for all countries, rich and poor. The rich countries certainly grew richer from the globalization-fuelled growth of the 1990s, and the living standards of most people continued to rise. At the same time, a growing number of people in these countries were losing their jobs as companies moved their operations abroad in search of cheaper labor. The gap between winners and losers in the rich countries grew wider.

The richer countries were also facing competition from newly developing countries like the **Asian Tigers** and China, which spent far less on providing their people with health and welfare benefits. In order to compete successfully with these new rivals, the richer countries cut back the **benefits** they paid out to their own people. The poorest got less help than before. This has also increased inequality.

The rise of international corporations and banks that held such enormous power also posed a threat to national governments. They could no longer feel in complete control of their own countries. This is what the French government discovered in the early 1980s, when it tried to introduce a socialist program. International business began withdrawing **capital** from France, which reduced the value of the French currency. The government was forced to reconsider its program.

Keeping down costs

In Bob Dylan's song "North Country Blues" (1963), he tells the story of how a North American mine has been forced to close by foreign competition. The South American mine is more competitive because the local workers are prepared to work for very little pay.

That government, like most in the richer countries, was freely elected by its people. Yet its wishes were simply denied by the interests of an international business community that no one had elected. Understandably, an increasing number of people were beginning to believe that globalization had serious consequences for **democracy.**

Consequences for the poorer countries

If the governments of the rich countries could be frightened by the new powers of the international economy, then what hope did the governments of the poor countries have? Their bargaining power was weaker than ever, and they found themselves forced to offer even greater rewards to the international corporations to set up on their home turf. Health and safety regulations were often ignored, **tax incentives** were occasionally offered, and protesters were quickly jailed. As a result, some of the new factories in the poor countries were similar to those of early Victorian England— full of very young employees working long hours for very low pay.

This was capitalism's dark side at the beginning of the twenty-first century. In some of these factories in the poorest countries, it was not uncommon to see young girls spending fourteen-hour work days making famous brand name goods for wages so low that they barely covered their food and board in an upstairs dormitory. The shoes and clothing they made were then sold by the local company to brand-name companies in the West. These companies went on to spend much more on advertising their brand names than they had on the actual goods. The profits were bigger than ever.

Consequences for everyone

Globalization has other results for the world as a whole. One is a greater homogeneity, or sameness, in the products that are bought and sold around the world. More and more, you find the same fast food restaurants, brand-name clothes and shoes, music, and fashions in the farthest corners of the globe.

The women in this factory in Zhongshan, China, are making brand-name tennis shoes for the Western market. They are paid a tiny fraction of the money that the shoes will sell for.

Western capitalism is so good at selling Western products that we are beginning to see a Westernization of the world. There is a serious danger that we will lose a lot of the world's cultural diversity in the process.

Another consequence is an increasing sense of uncertainty and insecurity. When jobs can be moved easily from country to country, few jobs are safe. When the world's economies are so interconnected, then bad news for one can sometimes mean bad news for all. An event like the terrorist attack on the World Trade Center in New York City on September 11, 2001, had economic consequences for almost every family on earth.

49

The world is becoming increasingly Westernized. McDonald's in Beijing, China, looks just like any McDonald's in North America.

A brighter outlook?

Capitalism's supporters argue that for all its problems and unfairness, the economic system of capitalism has still managed to raise the living standards of almost every community on earth over the last century. Its relentless pursuit of profit and production continues to create new goods, new industries, and new ways of looking at the world.

Capitalism also finds solutions to many of the problems it creates. For example, the Internet may prove to be as good for **democracy** as the power of the multinational corporations has proved to be dangerous.

New and democratic international political groupings may rise up to challenge the undemocratic powers of the world economy. The increase of protests against famous brand names for their **exploitation** of workers in poorer countries may persuade corporations (who are very image conscious) to change their ways.

Some companies are using the power of capitalism to combat the Westernization of the world and to help spread wealth to poorer countries. These companies act as agents for people in poorer countries who create crafts, art, and foods. The agents then sell these goods—which help spread knowledge of the poorer countries—to buyers in wealthier countries, and return almost all of the **profit** to the people who created the goods.

Also, poorer countries are being encouraged to participate in eco-tourism. Governments are finding out that tourists are willing to pay large amounts of money to visit, for example, rainforests. The money the governments receive from this eco-tourism means that they do not need to cut down the rainforests in order to make money and provide jobs for their citizens. Travelers who take an eco-tour to a poorer country are helping to put money in that country's economy, and are not harming the environment.

Global capitalism is a fairly new development. Like national capitalism in the nineteenth century, it will need to adapt creatively if it wishes to survive.

So, What is Capitalism?

Capitalism is an economic system in which private individuals or groups use private **capital** and labor to produce goods and services. These can be sold at a **profit** in a competitive **free market** that is open to everyone. As a manner of performing economic transactions, capitalism goes back more than a thousand years. As the dominant force in a given society, it only goes back as far as the eighteenth-century. During that century and the next, it slowly tightened its hold on the economies of North America and Western Europe, and over the last hundred years it has spread throughout the world.

Until the late 1980s the Pudong District of Shanghai, China, was mostly farmland. Today it has been transformed into a stunning new city, thanks to the wealth brought by capitalism.

History and politics

The truth about capitalism is that, left alone, it tends to generate wealth and inequality at the same time. Everyone on earth has benefited, at least to some degree, from the generation of wealth; but the generation of inequality has led to many social and political problems.

Throughout capitalism's history there has been an endless search for compromise, between setting it free to make wealth and holding it back with government regulations to curb the inequality it can produce. Without government intervention, those who work for pay—and who supply the labor that turns capital into goods and services—have usually been given an unsatisfactory share of the wealth that they are the most responsible for creating.

This was particularly obvious during the **Great Depression.** Afterward, government intervention in the capitalist economies was at its height. The opposite occurred in the 1970s, '80s, and '90s. It was then considered that government intervention had gone too far, and had become a brake on growth. Restrictions were lifted, economies deregulated, and capitalism let off the leash once more.

Generally speaking, it has been governments of the **left** that have favored intervention and governments of the **right** that have taken their feet off the brakes, but a capitalist system can operate under any government that allows economic freedom to flourish. It is harder to make this work in a situation where there is no political freedom, but it is possible. This has been shown by many military governments over the last few decades. Capitalism tends to favor political freedom, but it can do without it.

The only serious attempt to abolish capitalism—to rip it up by the roots—took place in Soviet Russia and those **communist** states like China which followed its example. Some of capitalism's faults were dealt with—guaranteeing every citizen a job, for example, which banished the fear of unemployment—but overall, the communist experiment was a terrible failure. The replacement of private property and the free market with government planning lessened economic efficiency and took away people's freedom.

Protests and prospects

Communism's collapse at the end of the 1980s left capitalism the dominant global economic system, but there was little time to enjoy the applause. The gap between rich and poor was widening. Environmental issues needed attention. Globalization was not only making these problems worse, but also creating new ones. Through the 1990s, a campaign of protest gathered momentum as people, angered by **exploitation** in the poorer countries, or worried about threats to democracy and the environment, came together in a loose alliance against the negative aspects of capitalism.

Many believe that all these issues have a common thread: capitalism's basic heartlessness. They feel, in the words of one famous phrase, that capitalism "knows the price of everything and the real value of nothing." Most accept that capitalism remains the most efficient generator of wealth, but they point out that the system itself has no interest in helping the less fortunate. Individual capitalists may have such an interest, but it is the desire for profits, and not the desire to help others, which drives

Protesters clash with police in Genoa, Italy, during a summit meeting of the world's richest nations in 2001.

the growth machine forward.

Since capitalism has not yet supplied its own conscience, society must provide one for it. **Socialism** has tried to supply a conscience, pushing for more equality as capitalism pushes for less, but socialism has been tarnished by the record of its more extreme cousin: **communism.** It remains to be seen where competitive, individualistic capitalism will find the conscience it will need in the twenty-first century.

Contrasting views on capitalism

Capitalism has always provoked controversy and strong opinions. Sylvia Pankhurst, a British campaigner for women's suffrage, vowed to "fight capitalism even if it kills me." She felt it was wrong that "some people should be comfortable and well-fed while others are starving." By contrast, British Prime Minister Winston Churchill remarked that only socialists thought it was wrong to make a profit—the real crime was to suffer a loss.

In the United States, President Eisenhower spoke admiringly of "the creative magic of free labor and capital," but his fellow countryman, the African-American leader Malcolm X, was not convinced. "Show me a capitalist," he said, "I'll show you a bloodsucker."

Timeline

1492	Columbus sails to the Americas
1500–1800	Age of commercial capitalism
early 1500s	Birth of **Protestantism**
mid-1700s	Beginning of **Industrial Revolution** in Britain
1764	James Hargreaves invents spinning-jenny textile machine
1767	Richard Arkwright invents water frame textile machine. Adam Smith's *An Inquiry into the Nature and Causes of the Wealth of Nations* is published
1832	Reform Act increases the number of those allowed to vote in Great Britain
1833	First Factory Act to regulate working conditions is introduced in Great Britain
1848	Karl Marx and Friedrich Engels's *Communist Manifesto* is published
1851	The Great Exhibition is held in London
1860s	Worldwide growth of **socialist** parties
1867	First volume of Karl Marx's *Capital* (*Das Kapital*) is published
1870–1914	United States and Germany overtake Great Britain in industrial production
1890	Introduction of **anti-trust laws** in the U.S. (Sherman Act)
1908	Introduction of the Ford Model T, the first mass-produced car
1914–1918	World War I
1917	First **communist** revolution takes place in Russia
1918–1919	Treaty of Versailles agreed in Paris
1928	Soviet leadership introduces overall economy planning
1929	**Great Crash** on New York Stock Exchange (October)
1929–1933	Worst years of the **Great Depression**
1933	President F. D. Roosevelt introduces first New Deal measures
1936	J. M. Keynes's *General Theory of Unemployment, Interest and Money* is published
1939–1945	World War II

1945	World Bank and International Monetary Fund (IMF) is set up
1947	**Cold War** begins. Britain recognizes Indian independence (start of European decolonization)
1948	General Agreement on Tariffs and Trade (GATT) formed
1949	Founding of the People's Republic of China
1950–1975	Capitalist economies boom in North America, western Europe, and Japan
1957	European Economic Community (EEC) founded
1959	Cuban Revolution
1961	Julius Nyerere becomes leader of Tanganyika (later renamed Tanzania)
1963–1975	U.S. involvement in Vietnam War
1968	Season of anti-capitalist protests in France
1973	Sharp rise in price of oil helps to slow down capitalist economies
1974	Friedrich von Hayek wins Nobel Prize for Economics
1976	Milton Friedman wins Nobel Prize for Economics
1978	Deng Xiaoping introduces market reforms in **communist** China
1979–1990	Margaret Thatcher is prime minister of Britain
1981–1989	Ronald Reagan is president of the U.S.
1989–1991	End of communism in Europe
1992	European Economic Community (EEC) becomes European Union (EU)
1993	United States, Canada, and Mexico form North American Free Trade Agreement (NAFTA)
1995	World Trade Organization (WTO) is set up as successor to GATT
1997	Kyoto Agreement made to control emissions that cause global warming. Economic slowdown begins in **Asian Tiger** economies
1999	Major anti-capitalist protest in Seattle
2001	Terrorist attack on New York and Washington
2002	Protests outside meeting of finance ministers at World Bank-IMF in Washington, D.C.

Sources for Further Research

Books

Downing, David. *The Great Depression*. Chicago: Heinemann Library, 2001.

Forte, Imogene, and Marjorie Frank. *Global Studies*. Nashville, Tenn.: Incentive Publications, 2002.

Grant, R.G. *Capitalism*. New York: Raintree Steck-Vaughn, 2001.

Grolier Educational Staff. *The War Years and Economic Boom, Vol. 6*. Bethel, Conn.: Grolier Educational, 2001.

Oleksy, Walter. *Business and Industry*. New York: Facts on File, 1996.

Ritchie, Nigel. *Communism*. New York: Raintree Steck-Vaughn, 2001.

Ross, Stewart. *The Industrial Revolution*. Danbury, Conn.: Franklin Watts, 2001.

Stein, Paul. *Global Warming: A Threat to Our Future*. New York: Rosen Publishing Group, 2001.

Taylor, David. *The Cold War*. Chicago: Heinemann Library, 2001.

Websites

http://www.imf.org

http://www.wto.org

http://www.epa.gov/globalwarming/

http://usinfo.state.gov/usa/infousa/trade/tradeovr.htm

http://www.doc.gov/

http://www.citizen.org/trade/

Key Figures in the History of Capitalism

Ford, Henry. (1863–1947). Ford was the American engineer who founded the Ford Motor Company in Detroit in 1899. Nine years later he was the first manufacturer to introduce assembly-line production for his famous car, the Model T.

Friedman, Milton. (1912–). Friedman was a professor of economic science at the University of Chicago from 1946 to 1983. He championed the **free market,** saying that government intervention in the economy should only be allowed to control **inflation** by limiting the amount of money in circulation. Like von Hayek (see below), he found his ideas growing in popularity after the economic crises of the 1970s. Friedman won the Nobel Prize for Economics in 1976. He served as a policy adviser during Ronald Reagan's two terms as president (1981–1989).

Hayek, Friedrich von. (1899–1992). Von Hayek was an influential Austrian economist and political scientist. He held important academic posts in London, England, and Chicago, Illinois. In his most famous book, *The Road to Serfdom* (1944), he defended **liberalism** and free market capitalism at a time when government intervention in the economy was more popular. After the crisis of the capitalist economies in the mid-1970s, many people started to agree with his ideas, and in 1974 he shared the Nobel Prize for Economics.

Keynes, John Maynard. (1883–1946). Keynes was a British economist who served as an adviser to the British government during both World Wars. He criticized the Treaty of Versailles (the treaty that brought World War I to an end), correctly predicting that the decision to make Germany pay **reparations** would be disastrous for the whole international economy. Throughout the 1920s and 1930s, he argued for increased government intervention to spur economies on and reduce unemployment.

Lenin, Vladimir Ilyich. (1870–1924). Lenin was the leader of the first **communist** revolution: the second Russian Revolution of 1917. Once in power he took the first steps toward the abolition of capitalism . He vastly reduced private property rights and the operations of a free market.

Marx, Karl. (1818–83). Marx was the German **philosopher,** economist, and political scientist whose theories of social development helped to inspire both **socialism** and communism. His most important work was *Capital (Das Kapital),* which examined capitalism in detail and predicted its inevitable downfall.

Reagan, Ronald. (1911–). Reagan was an actor who later turned to politics. He became president in 1981, and was reelected to a second term in 1984. He pursued **right-wing** policies, cutting taxes (particularly for business and the rich) and reducing government spending on provision of **welfare benefits.**

Roosevelt, Franklin Delano. (1882–1945). Roosevelt was elected president at the height of the **Great Depression.** His administration introduced the New Deal, a series of policies which involved spending government money to boost the economy and provide work to the millions of unemployed people of the time.

Smith, Adam. (1723–1790). Smith was a Scottish economist and philosopher. He is considered by many to be the founder of modern economics. He was the first to champion the emerging system of free market capitalism, and his book, *An Inquiry into the Nature and Causes of the Wealth of Nations* (1876), is still important today.

Thatcher, Margaret. (1925–). Thatcher became Great Britain's first female Prime Minister (1979–1990). Her government, the most right-wing that Britain had seen in 50 years, championed free market capitalism and tried to reduce government intervention in the economy. The power of the **trade unions** was lessened, and publicly owned industries were returned to private ownership.

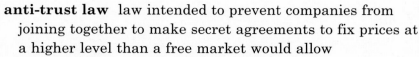

Glossary

anti-trust law law intended to prevent companies from joining together to make secret agreements to fix prices at a higher level than a free market would allow

aristocracy class of people born into families, usually wealthy, that also have a lot of political power

Asian Tigers countries in the Far East and Southeast Asia that experienced rapid economic growth in the late 1990s

benefits payment made by a government to those who are unable to work

capital money or other forms of wealth (such as land or machinery) which can be used to create goods or services

Cold War name given to the hostility between the free enterprise capitalist parts of the world and the communist parts of the world between 1947 and the late 1980s

colonialism system in which economically advanced and powerful countries rule over less powerful and developed areas

communism system in which property is owned communally (in common) rather than individually. The term "communism" later became associated with the system of economic planning that was created in the Soviet Union during the 1920s and 1930s.

democracy political system in which governments are regularly elected by the majority of the people, or a country in which this system exists

democratic taking into account the wishes of all people involved, often through voting

dictatorship government by an individual or a small group in which the majority of people have no say

Enlightenment period of the eighteenth century during which many European philosophers put more importance on reason and individualism than on tradition

exploitation taking advantage of, or using selfishly or unfairly

fascism dictatorial system of government originating in Italy; known for its belief that the country is more important than individual wants and needs

fixed capital capital used to turn working capital into products; for example, the machinery used to make goods

five-year plan a plan of all intended economic activity over a five-year period

free market market that government does not regulate, or only regulates a little

global warming gradual warming of Earth's atmosphere, which is mostly caused by rising levels of carbon dioxide gas

Great Crash sudden collapse of share values on the New York Stock Exchange in October 1929, which was a cause of the Great Depression

Great Depression period of great economic hardship that began around 1929, peaked around 1933, and lasted for most of the following decade. Most countries of the world were affected.

Industrial Revolution change from a primarily agricultural economy to one based on large-scale production in factories; this began in Great Britain in the eighteenth century

inflation increase in prices or increase in the supply of money (which leads to an increase in prices)

interest payment money repaid at regular intervals on a loan

interest rate the extra amount charged for being allowed to take a loan

investment putting money into a project in the hope of making a profit

left (-wing) in politics, usually associated with policies that place the needs of the whole community above the short-term wants of individuals

liberalism in the nineteenth century, a belief in the free market, free trade, and the removal of obstacles to either

multinational corporation large business that operates in several countries

philosopher someone who thinks, and often writes, about the pursuit of wisdom

privatization returning publicly owned companies to private ownership

profit difference between what is paid out and what comes back. For example, if an orange is bought for ten cents and sold for fifteen cents, the seller makes a profit of five cents ($15 - 10 = 5$).

Protestantism name given to the form of Christianity that split off from the Western Catholic Church in the sixteenth-century Reformation

public ownership ownership by the people as whole, as represented by the government

Reformation sixteenth-century movement for reform in the Christian church which resulted in the split between Catholicism and Protestantism

reparations payments to make amends for war damage

revenue in a business or country, the money coming in

right (-wing) in politics, usually used to describe people and policies which favor individual interests over those of the community

share certificate that people buy, which represents a piece of a business entitling the holder to a share of the profits

socialism set of political ideas which favor the needs of the community as a whole over the short-term wants or needs of the individual

tariff charge for bringing goods across international borders

tax money paid to a government

tax incentive reduction of the money demanded by a government from a business, with the intention of encouraging the business to set up in a particular place

trade union organization formed to protect the pay and conditions of workers

unemployment benefit money paid out on a regular basis by a government to the unemployed

universal suffrage all adults having the right to vote

welfare benefits money or services given to those who are unable to support themselves fully

working capital capital—such as raw materials—used up in the creation of products

World Trade Organization (WTO) international group founded in 1995 to regulate international economic activity

Index